CONTENTS

1	Introduction	Pg 1
2	The hustle	Pg 3
3	You have no Ikea	Pg 6
4	Traffic jam	Pg 9
5	Three pillar targeting	Pg 12
6	The ASAP system	Pg 17
7	Six-figure launch pad	Pg 27
8	How to get your very first sale in seconds	Pg 38
9	My little black book of contacts	Pg 41
10	Closing	Pg 46

Fashion Fortune: A Short Guide To How Entrepreneurs Can Build a Profitable Clothing Brand Without Breaking the Bank

Warren Young

Copyright © 2024 Warren Young

All rights reserved.

ISBN: 9798335200288

1 INTRODUCTION

Hi, I'm Warren. This book is the ultimate branding blueprint.

We're all about creating results.

Creating new products that get you bigger and faster results.

I have a background in music and started composing and writing music around 13 years old. I've worked with many UK and US artists, including 50 Cent, Marques Houston, So Solid Crew, Skepta, and Wretch 32, to name a few.

It wasn't until around age 20 that I decided to take a break.

I was burnt out and had little money in the bank from managing my money poorly. I was also expecting my first son, so I decided to get a job in retail and selling property and jumped into marketing. I had done those things for about five years.

Around the age of 25, I found a gap in the market and combined everything I learned from retail, from selling properties and in marketing, to applying it to We Brand You.

My older brother and I launched our company in 2015

And this year, along my online marketing journey, I've celebrated my 14,000th customer, which I'm super proud of.

The lesson and a significant takeaway from my story so far that I will say to anyone and share all the time is, 'Take breaks, but don't quit.'

When I was 20, things felt like they couldn't get any worse. I felt like I was taking a backward step. I felt the pressure to put food on the table for my family. But I didn't quit. I found myself and got back in the game at age 25.

As I said, I'm celebrating my 14,000th customer this year. So, I want to show you how you can do the same, take control of your situation, and multiply your results.

2. THE HUSTLE

Our mission and vision are to be the world's number one online academy for clothing brand startups, engaging, growing, and expanding your products and services internationally.

I quickly found there are not many companies or brands that are dedicated to clothing brands. To help them build a clothing brand and earn a fortune selling t-shirts, caps, and tracksuits

How was it done? These are some of our wins, some of the cool things that we've been able to do.

We've worked with Link Up TV, Mixtape Madness, Geordie Shore, MTV, many celebrities, and many artists—too many to mention here.

We also worked with Wembley Arena to create merchandise for their concerts and tours.

We worked with many different clothing brand startups and over a thousand different upcoming clothing brand startups.

Now, here's where I found the biggest problem. Out of everyone we worked with, 80% of clothing brand startups would not return to place a repeat order.

I'll say that again. 80% of the clothing brands we worked with wouldn't return a second time and place a repeat order.

Why is this? Most clothing brands don't know what they're doing.

I don't know if this is you or someone you know, but you get an idea, start making t-shirts, try to sell them to your family and friends, start an Instagram page, and then it dies out.

If you don't get any sales, you're left with all of the stock in your house, in your bedroom, taking up space. You've lost money, feel embarrassed, and don't know what to do.

You've told everyone your dreams of what you want to do with your brand, but you've failed, so you don't go back to place another order because you've quit.

Having a low customer return rate sucked for us because we weren't constantly making a profit from our customer base, and it sucked for our customers because they were failing. They were wasting money.

So we would then be on the phone with them, asking if they would like to place another order, but they'd reply, "No thanks; I've still got to stock from my first order."

So, after hearing that repeatedly, we started to feel their pain, and we knew where we needed to shift our focus and where we could be of the most service.

We realized we were better off shifting our focus from just being a printing and embroidery company (which there are so many of them out there anyway.

If you go to your local high Street, you'll see hundreds of them) to being a coaching and online academy dedicated to coaching and educating inexperienced clothing brands on how to build a clothing brand from scratch to six figures

This book is designed to provide the solution to no longer having wasted inventory, wasting your money, and pissing it down the drain. No more begging friends and family to buy from you, no more feeling like a failure, and no more wasting time.

Life is too precious to waste it on things you know nothing about and are destined to fail from.

All you need is a coach; like the great phrase legendary speaker and author Jim Rohn once said, 'Success leaves clues.'

3 YOU HAVE NO IKEA

My philosophy can be compared to the IKEA concept.

Imagine you go to IKEA. You're shopping with your partner, friend, or whoever it is and trying to find wardrobes for your bedroom.

You buy it, you go to the checkout, you purchase it, you take it home, and now you guys take it out of the box, and you start trying to put it together.

But you find that there is no manual inside the box. Will you be able to put that wardrobe together successfully?

Now, you might be able to. But I didn't have the manual when I bought a desk from IKEA in the past, so I ended up putting the backboard on the wrong way.

It got to a point where I thought, let me just leave it. It looks okay, anyway. But most people are trying to put their clothing brand together without an instruction manual, without knowing exactly what to do.

So they end up doing it wrong, leaving it, forgetting about it, or trying to create a brand and sell it, and it feels wrong.

Customers are coming to your brand and not getting the right feeling because you've set it up wrong. Instead of trying to assemble the wardrobes or put together this clothing brand by yourself, you need a manual.

You could put it together yourself, but it'll take a lot more time, waste a lot of energy, and need clarification half the time.

Something usually taking about half an hour will take three or four hours. And even when it's complete, like when I put my desk together, it might be wobbly, unstable, or even dangerous.

You must use an instruction manual. However, in today's market, new clothing brands do not have instruction manuals.

So, when we shifted our focus, we looked at what was out there that could coach you and give you a step-by-step walkthrough on how to create a six-figure brand from scratch.

On the path to success, so many different clothing brand startups are trying to grow in today's market, and you're one of them. You're probably doing it the long and hard way.

As I said, we've designed this manual to give you clear instructions and direction on assembling your clothing brand from scratch to six figures, with no more guesswork, confusion, or time-wasting.

There is a blueprint to follow, and this is that.

Now, we can't guarantee results. We can guarantee that our systems work only if you work.

You have to commit to it, follow it through hard work and discipline, be teachable, be willing to learn and dedicate yourself to not just learning this manual but going through it repeatedly and applying what you learn.

If information were enough, we'd all be rich, skinny, and healthy, but sadly, that isn't the case.

Action is the bridge between information and results.

Don't just learn it; put it into action as well.

4 TRAFFIC JAM

There is a good saying I like, and it goes, "Why get stuck in traffic toward your goal when you can drive down the fast lane to success?"

We like to think of this book, this information, and this system as the fast lane to success.

We've worked with so many other brands in the past, sat down, consulted with them, and managed to get them huge results based on this system we're now sharing.

If you follow the same system and dedicate yourself to it, there's no reason you can't drive down the fast lane to success, too.

Let's talk about the market.

The clothing industry is a 4.6 billion-pound industry worldwide, and you have to be aware of the potential.

There will always be a need for clothing in this world. There isn't always going to be a need for technology because technology comes and goes.

There were tape cassettes, then CDs, then DVDs, and now most people listen to music on digital download or streaming.

The same is true for cars; cars are constantly evolving. The three things that usually stay the same are houses, food, and shelter.

They may change slightly in design, etc., but there will always be a huge demand for clothing, food, and shelter.

Clothing is one of the big three. So, you need to position your clothing line in a way that speaks directly to your ideal buyer. So let's summarise:

we know there is a market, we know it's a profitable market, and it's growing year on year, and we know it's one of the big three

Now, you need to decide how to position yourself to speak to a specific person and convince them to become buyers. But we'll discuss that later.

Another word of inspiration that I love says this,

Treat your brand like a business, and it will pay you like a business; treat it like a hobby, and it will pay you like a hobby.

And guess what? Hobbies don't pay very well.

You need to treat your clothing brand like a business. Set it up with a good foundation so that it can pay you like a business.

Way too many startups make the mistake of getting started and only giving it a try. It's a hobby; they're just "seeing" if it works.

Don't just "see" if it works because chances are it won't.

Commit to it, treat it like a business, and it will pay you like a business.

5. 3 PILLAR TARGETING

We will dive into targeting and discussing how to attract your ideal buyer.

I was speaking to a client last week and asked him 'who is your target audience?'

And about 805 newbies replied, 'Everyone can kind of wear my stuff; my stuff is for everyone.'

I want you to avoid this.

They want to target everyone because they think it will mean more sales, but it does the opposite. In life, trying to please everyone ends up pleasing no one.

See, it's not about coming in and having a product that can fit everyone or suit everyone; it's not about that. It's about niching down, picking a specific set of people, and just catering to that specific set.

It's not about trying to cater to everyone because, like I said, you'll end up pleasing no one by trying to please everyone.

There are three pillars of effective targeting.

It starts with a:

- message
- story
- audience

What do I mean by this? A message is, for example, an apple a day keeps the doctors away.

That's a message, like a philosophy or a saying.
And then, you want to connect a story with your message.

For example,

I've been working 9-5, and my health has deteriorated. I was working double shifts, and I got burnt out. I went to the doctor, and my doctor said I had low health. And my doctor joked and said, "You know what? You need to start with an apple daily and start looking after yourself and caring for your health."

So, I then decided to create a clothing brand as a symbol of inspiration for myself and others to take care of their health while grinding before it's too late.

This is an example of a compelling story that compliments the message superbly.

The beauty of this process is that the audience jumps right off the page once your story is nailed. In this case, the target audience would be 'people who have 2 jobs or work double shifts that eat poorly and neglect their health to make money instead.'

So now you've got your message, story, and audience.

Your message is an apple a day keeps the doctors away. Your story is, your double shift, you got burnt out, the doctor said, start with an apple a day, and you've got your audience.

People like you, fellow nine-to-fivers burning out their health, must stop and take care.

You might think, 'Yeah, but this sounds nothing like a clothing brand. I just want to make quality clothing.'

You can make quality clothing, but people don't

just buy clothes for the sake of it. They buy clothes because of the message embedded deep inside the brand.

People don't buy Nike just because it's Nike. Nike is just a tick. It's nothing; it's the message behind it: Just Do It.

Nike inspires action. It motivates and moves you to take action and do something with yourself. That's what you're buying into on a deep subconscious level.

Most people don't realize this. It's the brand, like Apple, that Apple ogi that people buy worldwide; they inspire technology and advancement.

So you're not just buying a laptop; you're buying that cool, trendy thing. When you go to a coffee shop and see someone sitting on their laptop with an Apple logo on it, they're inspiring the future, moving forward. It's the feeling of belonging to the small crowd of coolness.

So, it's all about understanding the psychological aspect of why people buy.

Another message, story, and audience example is my own story.

Message:

take breaks, and don't quit.

Story:

At age 13, I wanted to impact the world through music. At age 20, I had to quit my dreams and get a real job because I had a son, and at age 25, I returned and applied everything I had learned in my marketing and sales jobs to go on to launch my 4 online companies and impact thousands and thousands of people worldwide.

Audience:

Men aged 25 - 44 chasing their dreams, wanting to make something of themselves, but getting battered by reality. wanting to do something with themself. Wanting to challenge the status quo and provide for their family,

When you have your message, story, and audience, you don't even have to think about what logo it will be now or your designs.

You already have a feeling and an idea for where your artwork will go, as opposed to trying to figure out what the artwork should be first.

When you know your message, your story,, and your audience, the logo and artwork will naturally come to you based on the picture your story paints.

Here are a few other popular stories with clever messages and stories buried inside them

Toy Story—The message in Toy Story is that friends are for life. The story of Woody and Buzz demonstrates this.

A Bug's Life: The message in that story is that heroes are not about size. They're bugs, they're small, they go on a journey, and they're trying to defeat the grasshoppers.

Monsters Inc. - the message is things are not what they seem right. They're monsters, but being scary is only their job.

Last but not least, there is Finding Nemo. The message is that no ocean is too large to cross for the ones you love.

These are all massive films that we know and love. We know and love these characters, but the message we carry after watching a film stays with us.

So that is the message in these stories, and this is what I'm trying to drill into your head while you're starting your clothing brand start-up: understand your message, have a compelling story, and target a specific set of people who will resonate with your message and story so that you can sell to them.

It's really important that if you take anything away from this book, take away this: Understand your story, your message, and your audience, and I guarantee you that it will make everything else fall into place and make it so much easier for you.

6 THE A.S.A.P SYSTEM

I coined this system myself, the ASAP system. The ASAP system stands for:

Artwork, Supplier, Acquire, and Produce.

Now, as I said, once you've crafted your message, your story, and your target audience, you'll want to enter the ASAP system.

And the first step in the ASAP system is **artwork.**

You'll base your artwork on the three-pillar targeting system because you now have the foundation, direction, and theme for it.

S stands for suppliers. You want to hire a reliable supplier who will save you time, money, and energy.

The A stands for acquire, which means you always want to acquire a sample before buying. This is crucial. We've made tons of mistakes in the past and lost thousands of pounds by not following this rule.

You should definitely get samples before buying. It sounds simple, but you'd be surprised how many people get stung here.

And the **P is for produce**. You want to mass produce and then prepare for a launch.

Let's break down the ASAP system further.

A is for the Artwork. There are two ways you can do artwork. You can either hire someone professional to do it for you, or you can do it for yourself for free. I will always advise you to pay a premium because you'll get quality back.

So whatever you put into this clothing brand is what you'll get out. Like I said earlier, if you treat it like a hobby and try to design things yourself, it will pay you like a hobby.

If you treat it like a business and invest in it, you hire high-quality artwork, designers, graphic designers, and web developers, then you'll get a return, and it will pay you rewards in ways you couldn't imagine.

So, premium ways are to use Fiverr, Upwork, and Google graphic designers, or if you've got a friend who does artwork or graphic design, take on a referral.

If you don't have the budget for it and are trying to do it for free, you can use sites like Canva, download Photoshop, Easil, or Visme, or use both.

These are also remarkable websites for designing artwork, so don't be afraid to use them if you're on a budget. But if you want my opinion, it's always best to go for a premium service, but both systems work.

S stands for Suppliers. A question we always get asked is, "Should I find a supplier in my own country or overseas?"

Ultimately, you'll want to use both. But I'm going to show you how to use both effectively.

You want to use your own country first and then transfer everything overseas.

The good thing about your own country is that there's good communication, because obviously, you both speak the native country language, so you can get things done quicker, emails are done quicker, you're not going to go back and forth and spend so much time understanding and translating what your supplier is saying.

There is quicker shipping time, so something that will take you three weeks to arrive from abroad may take you two to three days to receive.

So you'll be able to sell more products, have a larger range, and always restock much quicker. But the benefit of going overseas is lower costs.

You're buying in bulk, and you'll be able to get it for under $5-$10, depending on the item.

You'll cut costs, which will mean more profit in the long run.

You'll also have access overseas to larger custom fabric selections, such as silks, cashmere, and many other material combinations.

Last but not least, they're going to have faster production times simply because they've got factories, they've got staff, and they're used to doing much higher run rates than smaller shops in your country because, ultimately, many of these overseas factories are located in manufacturing districts.

Homeland and overseas have pros and cons, but I always advise you to find a local supplier when you're coming up and then transfer everything over overseas.

For example, once you're selling 10,000 in revenue per month, start looking at ways to get it overseas, like Pakistan, India, and China, to increase your margins, access more different fabrics, and grow in that space.

Slowly work yourself up, and then once you're in the big leagues and want to do more, you want to grow and expand: find a good supplier overseas.

If you want access to suppliers overseas, we have a quality product on our website called The Clothing Connect Manufacturers list.

So this is a direct list of all of -- Let's be real. The manufacturing industry is full of sharks; it's brutal.

I could tell you, my partner and my wife, like we can sit down and tell you stories of the number of times we've been stung by manufacturers abroad.

They have different ways of doing things; many are just money-hungry predators.

They will run off with your money if you're not careful. That's why we created The Clothing Connect to help navigate the industry.

It's like a little black book of our leading suppliers that we've worked with, I think 15 - 20 different manufacturers in there, Turkey, India,

China, and reliable suppliers that you can reach out to, hit them up, emails, phone numbers, and message them and place orders confidently.

Now, get samples because, like I said, samples are crucial.

They give you a better way of doing things and lessen the chance of getting stung.

So I felt like it was important for us to do that for you, just to help you navigate the shark-infested manufacturers industry.

A is for Acquiring. This is where you acquire and order your samples.

Note: you always want to request a sample first and foremost, as I said. Always move the

As soon as possible, transfer the conversation to WhatsApp for faster communication.

Only order from reliable companies with more than five years of trading experience.

If you can find a company that has been trading for over 10 years, that would be even better.

But a minimum of five years of trading experience is essential.

You don't want to order from someone who just entered the game six months ago and is using you as a guinea pig or as a way to get their feet on the ground and find their way.

You're nobody's test dummy.

Only work with people who know what they're doing, as this will save you time and money.

Last but not least, you should ask to see photos of the sample before they ship because it's all good to receive a sample, but if you don't like it, you have to send it back to them.

Then, they'll have to send it back to you. Requesting a picture sample before they ship could save you a lot of time.

For example, if the zippers are out of place before they ship, the picture will show this, and you can say ``I didn't want you to put the zipper there; I wanted you to put the zipper on the back or the side," and they'll make the changes.

Get as much information in the photo as possible before they ship; it speeds up the process.

Alibaba.com is an online wholesale marketplace where you can buy products in bulk.

It's a massive place where they've got hundreds

of thousands of different products. And one of the things they have is clothing.

You have the choice of buying a single item if you negotiate with a supplier and they agree to sell you one item; not all the time they do, but you can get samples.

However, Alibaba's real benefit is working directly with a manufacturer.

Twenty years ago, you would have had to fly to these countries, go to the manufacturing districts, meet with them, sit down with someone to build a relationship with them and place an order, but nowadays, thanks to the internet, you can just speak to these manufacturers like it's nothing.

It's made it 10 times easier, and that's why, for the first time ever, we're seeing the most multimillionaires come up more than at any other time in the world because of the internet.

Having access and direct access to these sorts of things just makes you more profitable and allows you to make more money in the marketplace.

One thing to remember in Alibaba is to always make sure you find a company with trade insurance. Also, always pay within Alibaba so that you stay eligible for trade insurance.

Trade insurance is simply to protect you if you buy a product and the seller sends a wrong or damaged product.

Trade insurance is important because you can open a case and be covered to get your money back.

Now, should it be the be-all and end-all? No. But when you're getting started and a little unsure, it's always good to be covered by trade insurance.

One of the cool things about reaching out to suppliers is that we have an opening script message that works well.

Like I said, we're all about saving you time and money.

And this opening script has been perfectly crafted; we've used it for years. It's perfectly crafted fast to track the whole communication space of ordering products.

So it starts with:

Hello, my name is *insert your name here*, and I'm searching for a reliable supplier for XYZ. I came across your company in my research and wanted to get some further information about it. Then you put in your quantities and XYZ. So please get back to me as soon as possible with the above information. My email is XYZ, my WhatsApp is da da da da da. Thank you, and I look forward to hearing from you. Hopefully, I can place an order with your company.

Kind regards,
insert your first and last name here

P is for Produce. So once your sample arrives, what's next? It's time to PRODUCE, and the script below is the perfect script to order. Take it from samples to produce your next order and get the best deal.

So here it is:

Dear *enter companies name*,

We've received and tested the samples you've sent. I'm happy to say that the quality of the products was up to the standard we need to be able to use you as a supplier.

So now we are ready to place an order of high quantity, however, to meet our quality rules for purchasing from new suppliers, we would like to order 200 pieces rather than our usual amount of 500.

That way, we can test everything on a larger scale and get feedback from our returning customers.

Once this order is complete and everything goes well, we can use your factory as a primary supplier for all future orders. So please get back to me as soon as possible so we can arrange the order details.

Kind regards,
Your name.

This will allow you to move from the sample phase to the production phase.

With these things, you want to get a supplier. The supplier will always push you to place a more significant order.

Most of the time, they'll settle for a lower order as well, but they will try to push you. I have seen it time and time again.

They will make you feel like they won't work with you unless you place a big order, but trust me, you have to stand your ground and know that they will accept a lower MOQ.

That's what's so cool about the last script I mentioned.

It's key to almost making them prove themselves and sell you why you should work with them.

It's similar to the TV show The Voice. The artist sings, and then the judges turn their seats if interested and start selling themselves on why the contestant should choose them.

At that point, the contestant has all the power and control.

You want to be in a position of power all the time when you're negotiating; therefore, that script that I just showed you puts you as the person who's like:

"OK, tell me why I should work with you. Why should I choose your factory instead of the other 100 - 200 factories out there?"

That's what negotiation is always about and will always be about. It's about who has the leverage.

Who is in a position of power? The person in a position of power with leverage can negotiate better terms, conditions, and everything else.

You've had some previous contact with the company because you've gotten samples and ordered them, and your communication is good.

Because you're using our script, wink wink,

they'll now view you as a serious buyer with what we call 'buyer's intent.'

And that's the highest level of professionalism you can show any business or company. If you're showing buyer's intent - you're a serious buyer. People will treat you with professionalism all the time, and it puts you in a good position. So just remember that.

So that is the 'ASAP system'. We had a three-pillar targeting system, the 'ASAP system,' which consists of artwork, supplier, acquire, and produce.

Once you've finished the ASAP system, you're going into your six-figure launch pad.

We've created a pre-launch checklist, which you should tick off to ensure that you're on track to launch and profit from your business in the best possible way.

7 SIX-FIGURE LAUNCH PAD

Stage one of the pre-launch is when you want to choose your online store.

Shopify is highly recommended. I've worked with Wix, Square, Shopify, and WordPress. Hands down, Shopify is the best platform. I love their back-end system; you can see your stats and your traffic; it's just clearer.

I also love that Ka-Ching sound that goes off every single day. There is no better feeling.

I recommend Shopify.com to build your online store.

Stage two of the pre-launch is choosing a domain name that matches your social media.

So if your brand is called Chili Peppers on social media, you want to make sure that Chili Peppers is what it's called on your domain name because nothing's worse than people finding you on social media and then trying to type it into URL but can't find you because your names don't match.

You need to make a conscious decision to ensure that all of your social media and URL names match for maximum visibility and so that people can always find you.

Otherwise, you will lose sales hands down.

Stage three on a pre-launch is customizing your store OR hiring a web designer.

You can do the customization yourself, but again, I'd advise you to hire a professional.

When you hire a professional, you'll get professional results. If you try to do it yourself, you'll probably get mediocre to poor results most of the time.

Now, sometimes you can strike lucky. But if you don't know what you're doing, how can you guarantee that it will work?

So always invest, invest, invest.

I like to see it this way: When someone wants to

open a bakery, a law firm, an accounting firm, or a McDonald's franchise, they always go to the bank and take money from the bank to invest in these projects.

Since your clothing brand startup is a real business, this shouldn't be different.

If you want to treat it like a serious business, you need to borrow money, go to the bank, or whatever it is, or use your savings and invest in your clothing business.

Because guess what? Investments pay you a return. I often don't see people going to banks or lending money because they don't believe it will work.

And guess what? If you don't believe it's going to work, it's not going to.

Getting an investment, finding the money and doing these things prove to yourself more than anything and your subconscious that this will work.

Otherwise, you wouldn't have borrowed the money.

So, you want to set the foundation strong from the get-go.

Stage four in the pre-launch checklist is to add

clothing inventory to your store.

You don't have to always start with 10-20 different pieces. Start small, maybe:

- 1, 2, 3 different clothing pieces,
- good logos on them
- good designs
- add them to your store
- set the pricing right
- make sure you're competitive
- make sure you've sorted out your postage and packaging
- make sure you've got everything in place

so that when customers come to your store, they can buy.

You also want to take good pictures. You and your friends (or hire a model or an artist, your local photographer) can take some really good pictures for your website because a picture speaks a thousand words.

Be bold and use your phone, as most phones are HD nowadays.

You'll be able to get really good pictures from your phone, but again, don't be afraid to hire a professional.

Stage five is to set up a payment processor and

PayPal add them to your website. It's really simple.

Last, stage six is to launch the store and make sales. That's your six-figure launch.

Congratulations, you're ready to launch. You've got your website down, your clothing, the best prices because you've used our scripts, your message, your story, your target audience, everything set up, and you've adequately prepared yourself for success.

But this is the part where most people fail.

They depend on their family and friends to buy clothes or "support them."

Once you run out of friends and family to sell to, once you've finished posting on your social media to your friends and family, and no one supports you, you'll get angry with them.

Your nan didn't buy your jumper, so now you're pissed off at her; you stopped going around to your family's house on a Sunday because no one is supporting your vision, your dream.

And this is where people get angry, and they quit. They thought everyone would rush in and buy their clothes. But guess what, that ain't a sustainable business model,

Not by any stretch of the imagination, so there is no point. And this is what I said at the beginning: growing a clothing brand from scratch to six figures is a mindset thing.

It's all about getting rid of the poor mindset thinking and putting better things in place, putting a mindset in place. One of the things to do is not rely on your family or friends.

If they support you, whoopie, good on them, good for you. But rely on something other than them because it's not a sustainable business model.

As Paul Jang says, **traffic is king**.

Whoever controls the traffic is king. Now more than ever, online, if you can get loads of traffic to your website, you will make sales.

The average conversion rate online is about 2%, meaning out of 100 people that hit your website, out of every 100 on average, you're going to get 2 sales.

Now, I've seen websites with a 5% conversion rate, which means out of every 100, they get 5 sales.

But on average, you're looking at about 2%. Whether you're Argos, JD Sports, Footlocker, eBay, or Amazon, these websites average between 2% - 4%.

What a great world it would be if we had 80% conversion rates, meaning 80% of people bought. But it's not; that's just how it is.

It's the law of averages—it's just how it is. So, if you can control your traffic, you will make sales. It's a no-brainer. And it's called the 80/20 traffic rule.

So imagine owning a store and walking with me. Imagine you owned a store in an abandoned shopping complex in a deserted town.

Now that your shop is open, cobwebs are growing in every corner.

You've wasted much money on goods you've yet to sell. That's what it's like when your website has no traffic.

You've got a store in an abandoned complex in a deserted town, and cobwebs are growing all around your shop. That's what it's like to have an online store and not drive any traffic to it.

As a marketer, I—and any marketer—will tell you we're obsessed with traffic.

We're just obsessed with it. You need to get obsessed with driving people to your website.

But the good thing is that now you can pay for

traffic, so you can pay to get people to your website.

So if you spend $1 to drive someone to your website and they buy, you will always be in profit. So, if you spend 30 pounds, do this quick math.

You spent 30 dollars to get 100 people to your website, and you're selling a T-shirt for 25 dollars each.

Like I said, out of every 100 people, you're going to get roughly three sales. So if three people purchase one t-shirt at 25 dollars each, you've made 75 dollars from those three customers.

And like I said, you've paid 25 pounds for those 100 customers. So you've made 50 dollars profit, you've spent 25 dollars, you've made 75 dollars.

So 25 minus 75 is 50 dollars, and you've made a profit. That's how you have to see it. It's a simple formula: you pay for your traffic.

You don't want to bother your friends, and you don't bother your family because they've got kids to raise, work to do, food to cook, and families that they—don't waste time on them, running them down.

Simply go out and pay for traffic, invest in a traffic system, create a traffic source for your website, and make money. We've done constant coaching calls on this website alone because traffic is key; traffic is king.

So, this slide shows how to send insane amounts of traffic to your website and bank massive profits.

Now, one of the things you can do is run paid ads on social media.

So that's your Instagram, your Facebook, your Twitter, and your YouTube. Set up a five-dollar-a-day budget on all of these platforms, and whichever one brings you sales, you focus the majority of your time on that channel.

So, guess what if you set up Instagram, Facebook, Twitter, and YouTube?

Your Twitter will pop up, and it will give you the most sales because you'll be able to track all these things.

If it generates the most sales, then 80% of your marketing budget should now go into Twitter.

Leave the other 20% in the other channels and let it run because you'll be in a profit zone.

The second one works the same, except it's for Google ads instead.

So you set up Google Ads, which you set up so that when people are searching on Google, I don't know. Say they're searching for exercise equipment.

If you're a gym brand and have a gym clothing brand, your product can show up now.

Your t-shirt can show up in the search results. If someone is searching for exercise equipment, they may also be interested in exercise gear.

They might click your ad, come to your website, like the look of the t-shirt or like the look of the sports bra or whatever it is you've got there, and they might purchase it.

They might just leave and not care and go what the hell was that?

But guess what? They might stay and buy it if it's good enough and it convinces them to buy at a reasonable price or whatever. So, you want to pay for Google ads as well.

The third one is that you want to pay for fashion influencers to repost.

Whether it's 'The Only Way is Essex' or celebrities, singers, and music artists, we've all seen it. You can pay these people to wear your clothing.

Now, it's always going to be more effective than

paid ads because when you run ads on social media, you're showing your product to people who have never encountered your brand before.

So, there's going to be an element of distrust there.

They'll see and trust that your products are good because they've never tried them before; they don't know anyone who's tried them.

But if you use a fashion influencer, that influencer has access to thousands of people and their audience, and their audience trusts them.

That's why their audience follows them; they trust them. So, if you send a t-shirt to the influencer, they will want to promote it to their brand; it's simple.

We all know what a fashion influencer is; if you don't, check it out online. Sometimes, an influencer will just ask for the product.

You send it to them, and they will post it or sometimes want money. It just depends.

You have to work it out, negotiate, and come to a price that is good for you. Remember to stay in the profit zone.

Always try to remember to stay in the profit

zone and negotiate so you get the best price.

The fourth one is to post video content on YouTube, which is another good one.

So, if you have workout gear, you want to post it or work with a personal trainer to shoot videos of some exercises and upload them to YouTube; they'll be wearing your gear.

You can drop a link in the description box below so that people watching the video can go back to your website, click the link, and buy the gear that they can see.

You want to create content around your brand. As I said, if we use an apple a day to keep the doctor away, the analogy of the message earlier, you could post different nutritional tips to help people avoid burnout.

You could also help people stay fit while they're working so they're not neglecting their health.

Create content around these things, but subtly drop your clothing brand in those videos and the link in the description box below.

This is called content marketing; you're marketing your product through providing high-value content. It works like a charm.

I have a music blog too. Music is one of my passions.

I've got a music blog online called Thir13een.com (at the time of writing this - a buyer is acquiring this blog for a healthy profit.

Another advantage to building a clothing brand is that, at some point, you could be faced with an offer from an investor wanting to buy you out.

When it is that kind of situation - it's usually for a healthy profit) however, back to the blog, I drop loads of different content about music reviews and things like that.

And I have a link in the description box below, which drives them back to my website, where we sell products that help them sound better and become more.

It's simple. It's a simple process.

They like the content, so they want to get more and buy premium products to help them sound better and become more. It's a win-win for everyone.

Fifth on the list is capturing emails and sending discount codes twice a month. So, the first time you email is at the beginning of the month when everyone gets paid.

You send out the second one in the middle of the month when people usually get paid if they get paid weekly or bi-weekly.

Next is to run competitions and giveaways. Give away a few T-shirts, and get people to promote your brand.

The message is simple: To win a free T-shirt or a free tracksuit bottom, repost this image and tag two friends.

You'll find loads of people reposting your stuff and tagging their friends.

So you're increasing your awareness. Those friends see it and repost it, and then you'll get this kind of network of people who are reposting and tagging, reposting and tagging, and that is doing a lot of the promotion of your brand for you.

Most of the time, when people enter a competition, if they lose, they'll still go ahead and buy your product anyway because they already showed an interest in you and also in themselves and know they're interested.

So they'll be like, well, I didn't win the competition, but I still want the products, so I'll go and buy them anyway. It works. It works, hands down.

So it's a real, effective way of marketing your products.

Second to last, you should collaborate with other brands in your industry.

So, if you're into fitness, you can work with other fitness brands. If you're into urban wear, you can work with urban artists and music artists.

If you're into health, you can work with health nutritionists; whatever your target market is, find out what other things they like that you can link up with, and then everyone, both brands, can benefit from both audiences.

Last but not least, you should blog about the latest news in your industry.

You can use the video content that you post to YouTube. You can also post that to your blog, which will show up in Google, and Google will start indexing you and adding you to the search engines.

It's another way to build community, build content, and drive sales.

So, to send insane amounts of traffic to your website, these are my Bibles.

8 HOW TO GET YOUR VERY FIRST SALE IN SECONDS

I often say this. "If you can make 1 sale, you can make 1000 more".

but getting your first sale is the hardest thing. You're new to this, don't have many followers, and have never sold anything online.

I get it. I have been there. When I started selling online in 2015, I didn't get my first sale for months.

It was painful and frustrating, and I gave up multiple times.

After doing this online thing for years, I have figured out a few ways to quickly get you your first sale.

Once you get the first sale, you know the path to getting more.

Getting your first sale is the most important thing.

It will show you the way forward, and you will know where to focus your energy and money to get maximum results.

I'm writing this to help beginners make their first sale. Some of these methods are paid, and some are free. If you do them right, they will get you a sale.

Shall we begin? Let's go ...

INSTAGRAM SHOUTOUTS

Let's start with the easiest one.
This will get you your first few sales, guaranteed. Yes, you'll need to spend money, but most will not be profitable if you do it right.

Here are the steps
- Find a big IG theme page in your niche
- Pay them to do a story swipe-up post
- Send their followers to your sales page
- Make Money

The simplest way to make money. Let's get into the details.
Find a big IG theme page in your niche.

The page should be between 100k & 500k followers. Don't go for lower than 100k followers.

Also, don't go for a 1mn+ followers account. They'll ask for ridiculous money, and you'll not be profitable.

Don't look for personal influencer pages. You only want to work with theme pages now. Personal influencers charge a lot more money.

It could usually be more profitable as well. Pages between 100k and 300k typically charge around $20 to $40 per story swipe post (I use dollars because more pages are in the USA).

This is your sweet spot.

If you sell a low-ticket product (under $50), you should spend no more than $50 per post.

It's crucial to pick the correct pages. You don't want fake bot pages.

Use SocialBlade or a similar tool to ensure the pages you advertise are legit and have real followers.

Design a Killer Story Post

Go to Canva, pick an IG story template, and

design a killer graphic. Keep it simple. Only talk about the problem you're solving. Talk about a benefit (what your prospect will get from buying your product). Be as specific as possible.

Your graphic must have a text overlay. Don't just post an image. Significant, bold text overlay on a relevant image.

Don't write, "Check out this clothing new clothing brand." Too generic. Boring. You won't get many clicks.

Your text should say:

"We sell T-shirts that make your biceps look 3x bigger."

or

"Take home 2 extra girls this weekend with our latest T-shirt collection."

This is much better. You can improve it even further. Be specific. Be bold. The bigger the promise, the more link clicks.

This is not overselling. This is marketing. People want to hear big claims—bold claims. Make them.

This is how you get attention, which is the new currency today.

You aim to get maximum link clicks to your sales page. The better the graphic, the more link clicks.

Remember: Pay them to do a story swipe-up post. Send traffic directly to your product page.

Space your shoutouts to once per week. You need to know which page is bringing you the most sales. Whichever one brings you the most sales, reorder another.

Use them again until sales run dry. Then, find a new page to repost. Repeat this process repeatedly.

9 MY LITTLE BLACK BOOK OF CONTACTS

The clothing manufacturing industry is full of sharks, snakes, and every other money-hungry predator.

I entered the clothing industry 8 years ago and had the misfortune of meeting many of these 'predators' ourselves.

I lost tens of thousands of pounds in almost 2 years wasted.

How did we mess up so badly, I hear you ask?

It's simple. We had no connections, no contacts, and no idea what these money-hungry predators 'looked' or 'sounded' like.

After years of placing orders, ordering samples,

conference calls, hiring translators, escrow accounts, back-and-forth contracts….

….We learned how to navigate the industry, learned who to trust, and discovered the good from the bad, the nice from the ugly, and the fast from the slow.

Now, we share our little black book with you.

I'm giving you my connects to remove all the guesswork for you.

We want to help you avoid the same mistakes we made and prevent you from wasting your time and money on broken promises.

This guide will connect you to our best and most reliable manufacturing friends, who can help you bring your vision to reality and build your clothing brand.

PAKISTAN

BRH AMIN
Manufacturer & Exporter Of Sports Wears

Manufacture Sportswear & Gloves, Uniforms, Boxing, and Martial Art Equipment.

Contact Name: Rehmi Amin
Contact Email: info@brh-aminind.com
Contact Mobile/|Whatsapp: +92 334 8046513

PUW SPORTS
#1 US Apparel Producers

Cut and sew, embroidery, screen print, DTG, Private labeling, Professional branded packaging

Contact Name: Mr Puwki
Contact Email: puwsports@gmail.com
Contact Mobile/|Whatsapp: +92 3414819028

TRUE INDUSTRY
#1 US Apparel Producers
Manufacturer and supplier of a variety of custom-designed cut-and-sew apparel

Contact Name: Ahmed
Contact Email: info@alliedapparels.biz
Contact Mobile/|Whatsapp: +923098875390

SPORTS ENTERPRISE
Cut & Sew Specialists for apparel clothing.

Sports Enterprise specializes in manufacturing high-quality fitted sportswear. Different products are available on demand at a reasonable price and are of the best quality.

Contact Name: Sports Enterprise
Contact Email: enterprise.sports@gmail.com
Contact Mobile/|Whatsapp: +923013184827

IBRAHIM WEAR

Cut & Sew Specialists for apparel clothing

Manufacturing and supplier of women's clothes, men's gym wear, hats, and masks

Contact Name: Jalee
Contact Email: jaleesulehry@gmail.com
Contact Mobile/|Whatsapp: +923311335933

PIEL SPORT

Reputed manufacturers of Leather Gloves, Sports Equipment, and Leather Jackets

Manufacturing and supplier for regalia and sportswear - custom pieces

Contact Name: Ubaid Aslam
Contact Email: infor@pielsports.com
Contact Mobile/|Whatsapp: +923003079797

TURKEY

AEM TEXTILES
Clothing and textile manufacturer

Manufacturing and supplier leggings, shorts, joggers, sports bras, vests, tank tops, sweaters, and hoodies.

Contact Name: Ubaid Aslam
Contact Email: info@aemtextile.com
Contact Mobile/WhatsApp: +90 232 202 2925

KONSEY TEXTILES
Clothing and textile manufacturer
Textiles, clothing, and bulk materials

Contact Name: Konsey Textile
Contact Email: info@konseytextile.com
Contact Mobile/WhatsApp: +90 (232) 349 10 64
+90 (232) 349 10 74
+90 (232) 349 10 84

ATT CLOTHING
Clothing and textile manufacturer

Leading womenswear manufacturers in Turkey specializing in premium woven and jersey garment design,

Contact Name: ATT clothing
ContactPage:
https://attclothing.com/#!/contactus
Contact Mobile/WhatsApp: +90 (212) 232 31 32

CHINA

SHULIQI CLOTHING
Garment manufacturing Plant

Garment manufacturers in specializing in premium garments for e-commerce

Contact Name: Mark
Contact Email: contact via Whatsapp
Contact Mobile/whatsapp: +8613411954088

AOLA SHENZHEN
Garment manufacturing Plant

Garment manufacturers in specializing in premium garments for e-commerce

Contact Name: Jane Chen
Contact Email: contact via Whatsapp
Contact Mobile/whatsapp: +8613411954088

10 Closing

I don't stray away from these things at all. If you want to build a thriving clothing brand and earn a fortune selling t-shirts, caps, and tracksuits, this is how you do it.

Stop relying on your friends and family.

Do not do it! You don't need to embarrass yourself, and you don't need to.

Even if you get everyone to buy your product anyway, who will you use after that?

They can't get you to six figures; they won't be able to get you six figures alone.

You'll need to reach out to other people, and many people fail here because they just don't know how or they try and fail.

If you've tried these things in the past, go back and try them again.

Keep going back and doing it over and over again until guess what?

One day, it's going to work; one day, it's just going to work, and it will click for you. You'll understand why it wasn't working before and why it's suddenly working now.

That's the difference.

The trouble is if you've tried these things before and you haven't built a sale, it's because you didn't know what you were doing and you're trial and error.

In life, there's a time for sowing and reaping. Running these ads and doing these things is like sowing your seed.

You cannot expect to sow and reap in the same season.

When you plant a seed in spring, your sweet corn grows at the end of summer.

You do not plant sweet corn seed in the patch,

and then two weeks later, it's grown, and you're reaping, or a day later, it's grown, and you're reaping.

No! The time for sowing and reaping is in two different seasons.

You have to be patient, trust the process, and persist and be consistent until the results show up.

I can't stress that enough. If there's anything to take away from this book, it's that there's so much value packed into it. It's unbelievable.

I want you to read this over and over. Just take it in over and over. Then, go back after this and read it over and over again.

It's your manual, your Bible, your everything. Do not do anything else if you want to build a thriving clothing brand. Use these paid traffic examples as your Bible, and do not veer away from them.

Keep using them and doing them until the results show up for you.

I look forward to hearing from you and hearing your stories on how this book transforms your startup clothing brand.

Wish you all the best!
Warren

www.ingramcontent.com/pod-product-compliance
Lightning Source LLC
Chambersburg PA
CBHW071842210526